Popsicle Cookbook

The Best Homemade Popsicles, Fruity & Chocolate Pops, and Frozen Treats to Satisfy All Your Summer Needs!

Healthy and Easy Ice Pop Recipes for Kids and Adults

Kaitlyn Donnelly

Disclaimer

The recipes and information in this book are provided for educational purposes only. Please always consult a licensed professional before making changes to your lifestyle or diet. The author and publisher shall have neither liability nor responsibility to anyone with respect to any loss or damage caused or alleged to be caused directly or indirectly by the information contained in this book. All trademarks and brands within this book are for clarifying purposes only and are owned by the owners themselves, not affiliated with this document.

Images from shutterstock.com

CONTENTS

INTRODUCTION

Summer means fruit and berry season is in full swing. It's time to replace the usual creamy delicacy with healthy homemade fruit popsicles.

Making popsicles out of juice at home is easier than ever. Spend 10 minutes or less and get breathtaking refreshing desserts full-of-live vitamins. Collected for you in this book are fifty-five of the best homemade popsicle recipes. Inside, you will find ideas that tell you how to make incredibly tasty homemade fruity, chocolate, creamy and smoothy, veggie popsicles.

Pops with berries, fruit and even a Sparkling Champagne - this is not the desserts of fashionable places, but homemade popsicles, which you can easily make at home.

CHAPTER 1. The Basics of Popsicles

General cooking methods

Homemade fruit popsicles will help you escape the heat. Also, you will receive wholesome vitamins A, D, E, P, B, and minerals.

1. The easiest way to make fruit pops at home is to freeze fruit juice in a unique mold. After the liquid is slightly frozen, a wooden stick can be inserted into the mold.
2. The second method involves the preparation of berry ice pops. The mixture is poured into popsicle molds and then frozen.
3. There is a cooking option, but it is a bit more complicated. You need to blend the berries in a blender and add lemon juice (or one that is listed in the recipe). Place the sugar in a saucepan with water, bring to a boil, let cool, then add the berries. The resulting mixture should be poured into individual molds, and cooled in a freezer until full firm.
4. You can also make milk-yogurt fruit ice pops. For this, you need natural yogurt and milk. Whip yogurt and add juice or pureed fruit. The mixture must be frozen. Then add the juice and freeze again.
5. Also, you can prepare puree from fresh fruit. They must be thoroughly rinsed, then cut into small pieces, and rinsed again.Put fruit in the blender and blend until smooth. The resulting fruit puree is poured into molds or cups, sticks placed in the molds, then put in the freezer for 4-6 hours.

Types of Popsicles

In this book, you will discover different types of pops, from fruity to hidden-veggie. After trying a few, use recipes as inspiration, combining and mixing the flavors, playing with layers, and inventing new combinations.

Fruity pops: Fruit pops are prepared from fresh, ripe, sweet-smelling, in-season fruits. Sugar, honey, and flavorings are mixed in to make a sorbet-like base after the pureed mixture is poured into the popsicle molds and frozen until firm.

Chocolate pops: Chocolate popsicles can be made from melted chocolate chips, chocolate whipped in a yogurt mixture with cocoa powder, and with chocolate topping.

Creamy pops: Smooth, rich-tasting, creamy popsicles are prepared from a mixture of yogurt, milk, condensed milk or other dairy or non-dairy products.

Fusion pops: Innovative flavors and sometimes unusual, unexpected combinations using ingredients such as herbs, vegetables, and full-flavored liquids make for the best popsicles. Some, such as tequila pops, are best suited for an adult palate.

The secrets of fruit pops:

1. Use fresh fruits and berries.

2. Wash fruit thoroughly and remove any damaged areas. Make juice or fruit/berry puree immediately before cooking popsicles.

3. If you are preparing pops using syrup, use as little water as possible. The more concentrated the juice, the tastier it will be.

4. Popsicles made from sieved juice are more transparent but also denser. Pops made from fruit juice with pulp or from fruit/berry puree will turn out looser and softer and with a richer taste.

5. After preparing the popsicle mixture, pour it into silicone or plastic molds, and place it in the freezer. After 1-2 hours, when the mixture thickens, insert a stick into the center of each shape, and return to the freezer until it fully freezes.

6. If popsicle is difficult to remove from the mold, dip mold in hot water for twenty seconds.

7. If the treat is stored for a long time in the freezer, it may harden excessively, so eat soon after making.

8. Ice pops can be made from coffee and tea.

9. Make fun layered pops—for example, one of peaches, then the other of strawberries, and alternately filling them into the molds.

Homemade popsicles FAQ

"Can popsicles be made without a mold?"

You can prepare fruit pops in yogurt containers, cans, glasses, or even in a bread pan! If you have problems inserting sticks in these non-traditional shapes, firmly wrap the top of the mold with aluminum foil (try to prevent the foil from touching the mixture). Then poke the sticks through the foil, and they'll stand!

"How do you make popsicles that are soft?"

It all comes down to the molecular structure! Water freezes to ice, which is definitely not the ideal popsicle. However, if you start adding sugar, fiber from fruits or fat from coconut milk, the molecules can not freeze so neatly, and as a result, it will be a more fluffy, creamy popsicle.

"How can you make sugar-free yet sweet popsicles?"

You can make sugar-free fruit popsicles using either fruit puree (which contains natural sugars and fibers to preserve soft fruit pops), fat coconut milk, or Greek yogurt.

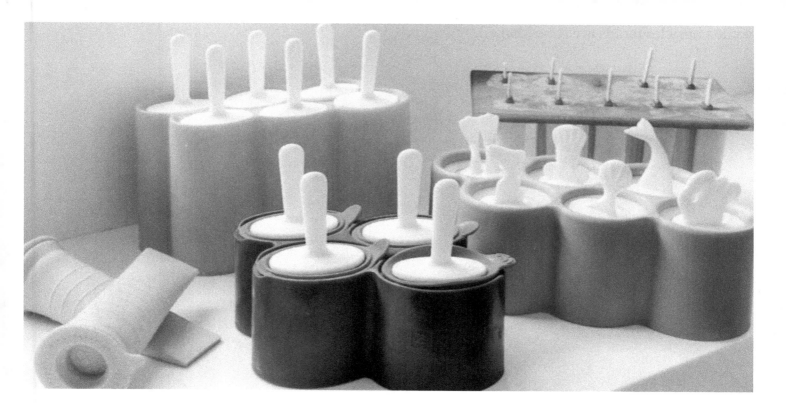

CHAPTER 2. Popsicle Molds

The essence of the silicone product is to maintain the shape of the pops. Prepared fruit mixture needs to be poured into a mold, sticks inserted, and put into the freezer for a few hours.

Silicone is flexible, and if it is a quality product, then popsicles can be easily removed from the mold. Most high-quality models withstand temperature drops from -60 to +230 degrees, which means that they can be used not only for popsicles and ice cream but also for baking. Many molds come as sets that include the popsicle sticks. Unlike tinwares, silicone cookware is an inert material and does not react with food.

Silicone forms can have different shapes

Molds can come in the form of fairy tale characters or animals. Children especially love to experiment with this product. They often come in bright colors, enticing children to cook with you and enjoy the finished product.

Some popsicles molds are cone-shaped.

While others are cup-shaped.

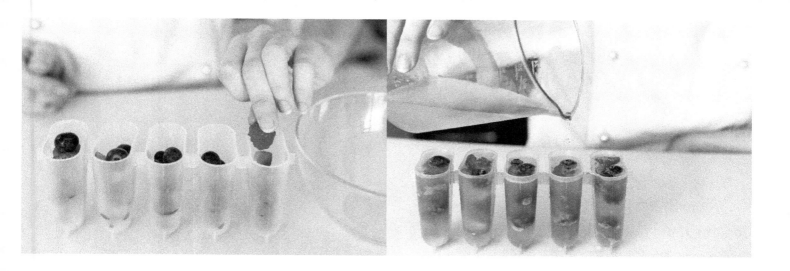

Cooking Process or How to Make the Best Popsicles

The usage of silicone forms is not complicated. Cooking popsicles consists of several stages :

1. Combine all the ingredients prepared for pops. Use a blender if necessary.
2. Pour the mixture into the silicone mold to the specified level, insert the sticks.
3. Put the molds in the freezer for 6-8 hours. It is recommended to freeze the popsicle in the evening; then in the morning, you can already enjoy the dessert.
4. Take out the popsicle molds from the freezer and gently remove the treat by the wand, gently pressing the bottom with your fingers, as if squeezing the briquette.
5. If the mixture is over-frozen and does not get from the mold, hold it for no more than a minute under hot water.

When making homemade popsicles using a silicone mold:

1. Do not be scared to experiment with recipes.
2. It is not necessary to blend the whole mixture—whole slices of fruit can be used.
3. For making popsicles with chocolate topping, remove the popsicles from the freezer, dip each pop in warm icing, lay out on baking paper, and freeze until chocolate has hardened.

CHAPTER 3. Recipes

FRUITY & CHOCOLATE POPSICLES

Mango and Cream

Prep time: 15 minutes (+6 hours)

Cooking time: none

Servings: 6-8

Nutrients per serving:

Carbohydrates – 17.4 g

Fat – 2 g

Protein – 6.7 g

Calories – 109

Ingredients:

- 2 cups fresh mango, diced
- ½ cup apple or orange juice
- 4 tbsp honey
- 1 cup coconut milk or cream, whipped
- ½ cup 0% fat coconut Greek yogurt
- 2 scoops collagen peptides/vital proteins

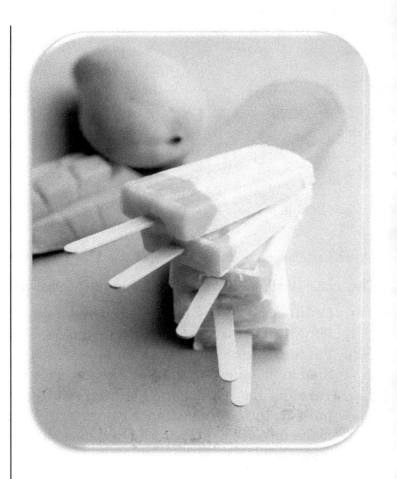

Instructions:

1. Puree mango, juice, and 2 tbsp honey in a blender. Pour into a jar.
2. To prepare coconut cream: place whip coconut milk, Greek yogurt, remaining honey, and collagen peptides in a blender. Blend until creamy and smooth.
3. Pour 3 tablespoons of coconut cream into popsicle molds and alternate wit 1 tablespoon of fruit mixture.
4. Add sticks and freeze approximately 6 hours.

Peaches and Cream

Prep time: 15 minutes (+6 hours)

Cooking time: none

Servings: 6-8

Nutrients per serving:

Carbohydrates – 22.4 g

Fat – 2.2 g

Protein – 7.4 g

Calories – 131

Ingredients:

- 2 cups frozen or fresh peaches
- ½ cup apple or orange juice
- 4 tbsp honey
- 1 cup canned coconut milk or cream, whipped
- ½ cup 0% fat coconut Greek yogurt
- 2 scoops collagen peptides/vital proteins

Instructions:

1. Puree peaches, juice, and 2 tbsp honey in a blender. Pour into a jar.
2. To prepare coconut cream: place whipped coconut milk, Greek yogurt, remaining honey, and collagen peptides in a blender and blend until creamy and smooth.
3. Pour 2 tablespoons of coconut cream into popsicle molds and alternate with 1 tablespoon of fruit mixture.
4. Add sticks and freeze approximately 6 hours.

Striped Tropical

Prep time: 10 minutes (+12 hours)

Cooking time: none

Servings: 8

Nutrients per serving:

Carbohydrates – 6.5 g

Fat – 0 g

Protein – 0.2 g

Calories – 26

Ingredients:

- ½ cup watermelon, seeds removed
- ½ cup guava nectar
- ½ cup passion fruit juice

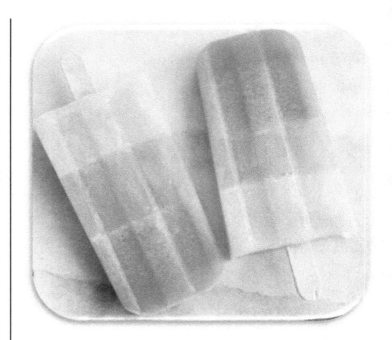

Instructions:

1. Process watermelon in.
2. Pour watermelon mixture into popsicle molds. Freeze for at least 4 hours, until fully firm.
3. Remove from freezer and fill molds with guava nectar. Add sticks and freeze another 4 hours, until firm.
4. Remove from freezer again and top with passion fruit juice. Freeze for another 4 hours, until firm.

Honey Lemonade

Prep time: 10 minutes (+4-6 hour)

Cooking time: 10 minutes

Servings: 8

Nutrients per serving:

Carbohydrates – 18.1 g

Fat – 0.2 g

Protein – 0.3 g

Calories – 72

Ingredients:

- 1 cup lemon juice
- ½ cup honey
- 1½ cup cold water
- 16 flowers eatable (optional)

Instructions:

1. Simmer honey and water in a saucepan until honey is melted.
2. Mix together the lemon juice, melted honey.
3. Add the edible flowers and pour mixture into molds.
4. Place sticks in and freeze 4-6 hours, until firm.

Banana Cream Pie

Prep time: 10 minutes (+4-6 hours)

Cooking time: none

Servings: 8

Nutrients per serving:

Carbohydrates – 12.7 g

Fat – 5.6 g

Protein – 2 g

Calories – 110

Ingredients:

- 2 slices frozen Marie Callender's Banana Cream Pie
- 1 cup milk or pineapple juice
- ½ cup vanilla wafers

Instructions:

1. Combine pie and milk or pineapple juice in a blender and mix until smooth and creamy.
2. Pour the mixture into the molds, leaving about a half-inch of space on top.
3. Crush the vanilla wafers into small pieces and top popsicles with these crumbs.
4. Add sticks to each mold, and freeze for at least 4-6 hours.

Coconut Mocha

Prep time: 15 minutes (+4-6 hours)

Cooking time: none

Servings: 10

Nutrients per serving:

Carbohydrates – 2 g

Fat – 16.5 g

Protein – 1.5 g

Calories – 165

Ingredients:

- 13.5 ounce can full-fat coconut milk
- 2 cups iced mocha coffee
- 5 tbsp shredded coconut

Instructions:

1. Combine coffee and coconut milk in a saucepan. Let cook, stirring, for 10 minutes.
2. In the bottom of each mold, place ½ tbsp of shredded coconut.
3. Pour the mixture into the molds.
4. With a butter knife, stir each popsicle.
5. Add sticks. Freeze for at least 4-6 hours.

Honeydew Melon Mint

Prep time: 10 minutes (+4-6 hours)

Cooking time: none

Servings: 10

Nutrients per serving:

Carbohydrates – 12.2 g

Fat – 0.1 g

Protein – 0.6 g

Calories – 48

Ingredients:

- ½ honeydew melon, cubed
- ⅓ cup granulated sugar
- 5-10 leaves mint
- 1 tbsp lime juice

Instructions:

1. Combine all ingredients in a blender and process until the sugar is completely dissolved and mint is well minced.
2. Pour the melon mixture into the molds, add sticks and freeze for at least 4-6 hours.

Kiwi Watermelon Fruit

Prep time: 10 minutes (+6 hours)

Cooking time: none

Servings: 8

Nutrients per serving:

Carbohydrates – 15 g

Fat – 0.5 g

Protein – 1.4 g

Calories – 64

Ingredients:

- 4 kiwi
- 3 cups watermelon, seedless

Instructions:

1. Process watermelon in a blender until smooth. Set aside.
2. Do the same with the kiwi, adding 1 tbsp water if necessary.
3. Pour the kiwi puree into the bottom of molds and freeze for about an hour.
4. Remove from the freezer and add the watermelon puree on top.
5. Add sticks and freeze for at least 5 hours.

Orange Vanilla

Prep time: 15 minutes (+4-6 hours)

Cooking time: none

Servings: 5

Nutrients per serving:

Carbohydrates – 16.3 g

Fat – 1.1 g

Protein – 1.9 g

Calories – 81

Ingredients:

- 6 oz orange juice concentrate
- 1 cup milk
- 1 cup water
- 1 tsp vanilla extract
- ¼ cup sugar

Instructions:

1. Mix all ingredients until the sugar is completely dissolved.
2. Pour the mixture into popsicle molds and freeze for 2 hours.
3. Add sticks and freeze for at least 4 hours.

Key Lime Pie

Prep time: 10 minutes (+4-6 hours)

Cooking time: none

Servings: 6

Nutrients per serving:

Carbohydrates – 12.3 g

Fat – 0.6 g

Protein – 2.8 g

Calories – 64

Ingredients:

- 1½ cups low-fat buttermilk
- ¼ cup key lime juice
- ¼ cup sugar

Instructions:

1. Blend all ingredients in a blender until smooth and the sugar is completely dissolved.
2. Freeze for 2 hours.
3. Add sticks and freeze for at least 4 hours.

Blood Orange and Creamy Coconut

Prep time: 30 minutes (+4-6 hours)

Cooking time: none

Servings: 10

Nutrients per serving:

Carbohydrates – 7.8 g

Fat – 7.9 g

Protein – 0.7 g

Calories – 115

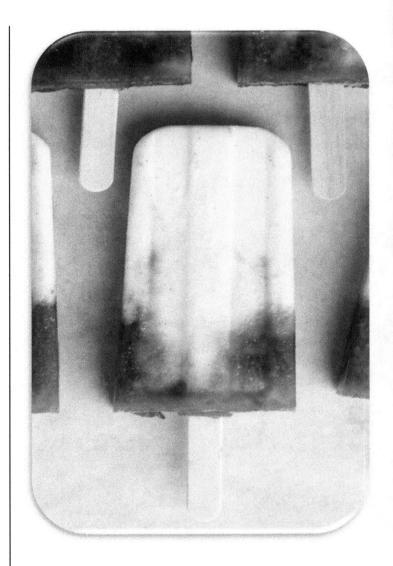

Ingredients:

- 1 (15 oz) can full-fat coconut milk
- 1 tsp vanilla extract
- 1¼ cups fresh blood orange juice
- ¼ cup light agave nectar/syrup

Instructions:

1. Whisk together coconut milk, vanilla extract and 2 tbsp of the agave nectar/syrup until smooth and creamy. Set aside.
2. In a second bowl, stir together the blood orange juice and remaining agave nectar/syrup.
3. For creamy pops: Combine the creamy mixture and juice mixture, and pour into molds. Freeze for 30 minutes. Add sticks, then freeze for at least 4 hours.
4. For layered pops: Pour the creamy mixture into molds and freeze for 10 minutes. Then top with the juice mixture. Freeze again for 30 minutes. Add sticks.,then freeze for at least 4 hours.

Striped Mango Coconut

Prep time: 15 minutes (+4-6 hours)

Cooking time: none

Servings: 10

Nutrients per serving:

Carbohydrates – 10.8 g

Fat – 5.9 g

Protein – 1 g

Calories – 94

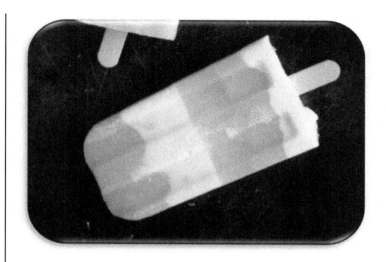

Ingredients:

- 1 ripe mango, diced
- 1¼ cup orange juice
- 1 cup coconut milk
- 1 tbsp granulated sugar

Instructions:

1. In a blender, puree ¾ diced mango and ¼ cup orange juice until smooth.
2. In a bowl, whisk together the coconut milk and sugar. Then add remaining mango and stir carefully.
3. Put 1-2 spoonfuls of pureed mango into the molds, then 1-2 spoonfuls of the coconut mixture, then 3-4 spoonfuls of orange juice into molds. Freeze for 45-60 minutes.
4. Remove from the freezer. Repeat the layers, Add sticks and freeze for another 45-60 minutes between layers.
5. When the molds are filled, freeze for at least 4-6 hours.

Dairy Free Coffee

Prep time: 15 minutes (+4-6 hours)

Cooking time: none

Servings: 10

Nutrients per serving:

Carbohydrates – 6.6 g

Fat – 0.9 g

Protein – 1.7 g

Calories – 43

Ingredients:

- 2 cups almond milk protein + fiber
- 2 tbsp dark brown sugar, divided
- ½ tsp vanilla extract
- 1 cup strong cold coffee
- Pinch of ground cinnamon (optional)

Instructions:

1. Whisk together almond milk, 1 tbsp brown sugar, a pinch of cinnamon and vanilla extract in a bowl.
2. Pour the mixture into molds.
3. Mix strong cold coffee with 1 tbsp brown sugar and stir until the sugar is completely dissolved.
4. Pour the coffee mixture into the molds.
5. Freeze for 30-45 minutes.
6. Add sticks, then freeze for at least 4-6 hours.

Frozen Hot Chocolate

Prep time: 15 minutes (+6-8 hours)

Cooking time: 10 minutes

Servings: 12

Nutrients per serving:

Carbohydrates – 12.9 g

Fat – 2.3 g

Protein – 2.9 g

Calories – 81

Ingredients:

- 4 cups milk
- 6 tbsp granulated sugar
- 2 tbsp semi-sweet chocolate chips
- ½ cup mini marshmallows

Instructions:

1. Combine milk, granulated sugar, and semi-sweet chocolate chips in a saucepan. Bring to a simmer, stirring constantly.
2. When sugar dissolves and the chocolate melts, remove from heat and allow to cool.
3. Put a few marshmallows into the bottom of molds.
4. Pour in cooled hot chocolate.
5. Add sticks and freeze for at least 6-8 hours until full firm.

Oreo Cookies Creamsicles

Prep time: 15 minutes (+4-6 hours)

Cooking time: none

Servings: 5

Nutrients per serving:

Carbohydrates – 13.9 g

Fat – 4.6 g

Protein – 1.7 g

Calories – 101

Ingredients:

- 4-5 Oreo Cookies
- ¾ cup whole milk
- 2 tbsps Sugar
- ½ cup cool whip

Instructions:

1. Blend milk, cool whip and sugar in a blender.
2. Add Oreo cookies and blend until cookies are broken into small bits.
3. Pour the cream-Oreo mixture into the molds. Freeze for 30 minutes..
4. Add sticks and freeze for at least 4-6 hours.

Cherry Coke

Prep time: 10 minutes (+4-6 hours)

Cooking time: none

Servings: 8

Nutrients per serving:

Carbohydrates – 18.9 g

Fat – 0.1 g

Protein – 0.4 g

Calories – 73

Ingredients:

- 16-20 oz cola
- 24 maraschino cherries, halved

Instructions:

1. Place 3-6 cherry halves in each mold.
2. Pour cherry juice in each mold to fill ⅓ of the way.
3. . Freeze for 3 hours.
4. Remove from freezer and pour cola in each mold, leaving ¼ space at the top of each mold.
5. Add sticks and freeze for at least 4 hours.

Hawaiian Cream

Prep time: 15 minutes (+4-6 hours)

Cooking time: none

Servings: 10

Nutrients per serving:

Carbohydrates – 13.6 g

Fat – 2.1 g

Protein – 0.9 g

Calories – 69

Ingredients:

- 1 cup fresh pineapple
- 14 oz lite coconut milk
- 1 banana
- 1 cup fresh mango
- 3-4 tbsp sugar

Instructions:

1. Whisk together all ingredients.
2. Pour mixture into the molds. Freeze for 30 minutes.
3. Add sticks and freeze for at least 4-6 hours.

YOGURT CREAMSICLES

Smoothie Fruit

Prep time: 5 minutes (+4-6 hours)

Cooking time: none

Servings: 10

Nutrients per serving:

Carbohydrates – 8 g

Fat – 0 g

Protein – 2 g

Calories – 39

Ingredients:

- 1½ cup orange juice
- ¾ cup light vanilla Greek yogurt
- 2½ cup organic frozen fruit of your choice

Instructions:

1. Blend together all ingredients.
2. Pour mixture into popsicle molds
3. Add sticks and freeze approximately 4-6 hours.

Raspberry Coconut

Prep time: 10 minutes (+4-6 hour)

Cooking time: none

Servings: 10

Nutrients per serving:

Carbohydrates – 4 g

Fat – 2 g

Protein – 0.2 g

Calories – 32

Ingredients:

- 1 cup full-fat coconut milk
- 1 cup plant-based yogurt
- 1 tsp vanilla extract
- 2 tbsp maple syrup
- 1 cup raspberries
- 1 tbsp dragonfruit powder (optional)

Instructions:

1. Blend coconut milk, yogurt, vanilla extract and maple syrup in a blender or food processor.
2. Add in raspberries dragonfruit powder, and blend until smooth.
3. Pour fruit mixture into popsicle molds
4. Add sticks and freeze approximately 4-6 hours.

Coconut Lime

Prep time: 10 minutes (+4-6 hour)

Cooking time: none

Servings: 10

Nutrients per serving:

Carbohydrates – 12 g

Fat – 2.9 g

Protein – 2.3 g

Calories – 81

Ingredients:

- 1½ cup vanilla Greek yogurt or coconut cream
- ¾ cup lime juice
- Zest of 2 limes
- ½ cup coconut cream

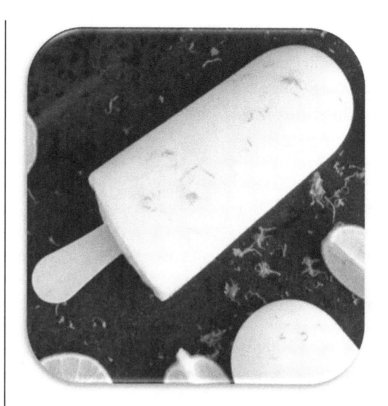

Instructions:

1. Blend all ingredients in a blender.
2. Pour the mixture into popsicle molds.
3. Freeze for 1 hour.
4. Add sticks and freeze approximately 4-6 hours.

Peaches and Cream Smoothie

Prep time: 9 minutes (+4-6 hours)

Cooking time: none

Servings: 10

Nutrients per serving:

Carbohydrates – 10.9 g

Fat – 0.5 g

Protein – 2.1 g

Calories – 53

Ingredients:

- 1 cup vanilla Greek yogurt
- 4 ripe peaches, sliced
- 1 ripe peach, chopped
- 1 tbsp honey

Instructions:

1. Puree peaches slices, yogurt, and honey in a blender.
2. Pour half of the mixture into molds, add thinly chopped peaches, then add the rest of the mixture.
3. Add sticks and freeze approximately 4-6 hours.

Cherry Chocolate Chip

Prep time: 30 minutes (+4-6 hours)

Cooking time: 10 minutes

Servings: 12

Nutrients per serving:

Carbohydrates – 28.5 g

Fat – 1.6 g

Protein – 1.9 g

Calories – 126

Ingredients:

- 4 cups fresh sweet cherries
- 8 oz cherry Greek yogurt
- ⅓ cup mini dark chocolate chips
- 1 cup granulated sugar
- Pinch salt
- ½ cup water
- Juice of ½ lemon

Instructions:

1. In a saucepan, combine cherries, sugar, water and salt. Bring to a boil, constantly stirring.
2. Remove from heat and allow to cool for 10 minutes.
3. Place the mixture in a blender, add lemon juice and blend until smooth.
4. Place ½ tsp of cherry Greek yogurt then 1 tbsp cherry puree into molds.
5. Sprinkle 1 tbsp mini dark chocolate chips into each popsicle.
6. Using the end of a spoon, mix until you start to see swirls.
7. Add sticks and freeze for at least 4-6 hours.

Vanilla Greek Yogurt Funfetti

Prep time: 10 minutes (+6 hours)

Cooking time: none

Servings: 8

Nutrients per serving:

Carbohydrates – 12.4 g

Fat – 2.9 g

Protein – 3.6 g

Calories – 88

Ingredients:

- ½ cup vanilla almond milk
- 2 cups vanilla Greek yogurt
- ⅓ cup rainbow sprinkles
- ½ tsp vanilla extract

Instructions:

1. Combine almond milk, Greek yogurt, and vanilla extract in a blender for 5-7 minutes.
2. Once the mixture is smooth, add sprinkles and stir gently.
3. Transfer mixture immediately to the popsicle molds, leaving about a half-inch of space on top
4. Add sticks and freeze for at least 6 hours.

Orange Creamsicles

Prep time: 10 minutes (+4-6 hours)

Cooking time: none

Servings: 6-8

Nutrients per serving:

Carbohydrates – 11.2 g

Fat – 11.5 g

Protein – 0.3 g

Calories – 159

Ingredients:

- 1 cup orange juice
- 1 cup heavy cream or full-fat coconut milk
- 3 tbsp honey
- ½ tsp vanilla extract
- ¼ tsp orange extract

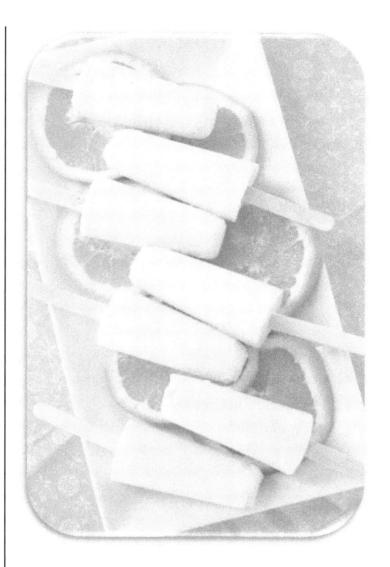

Instructions:

1. Whisk together all ingredients.
2. Pour the cream mixture into the molds.
3. Add sticks and freeze for at least 4-6 hours.

Peanut Butter Yogurt with Chocolate Topping

Prep time: 20 minutes (+6 hours)

Cooking time: none

Servings: 6

Nutrients per serving:

Carbohydrates – 36.8 g

Fat – 41.1 g

Protein – 18.5 g

Calories – 563

Ingredients:

For the popsicles:

- 1 cup smooth peanut butter
- ½ cup vanilla Greek yogurt
- ¾ cup milk
- 2 tbsp honey

For the topping:

- 1 cup chocolate
- 2 tbsp coconut oil
- 1 tbsp smooth peanut butter
- Salted peanuts, crushed

Instructions:

For the popsicles:

1. Whisk together all ingredients.
2. Pour the mixture into popsicle molds. Freeze for 2 hours.
3. Add sticks and freeze for at least 4 hours.

For the topping:

4. Melt chocolate in a microwave, add coconut oil and stir every 20 seconds.
5. Stir in the peanut butter. Set aside to cool for 5-10 minutes.
6. When popsicles are completely frozen, dunk each pop into chocolate. Sprinkle with sliced peanuts. Enjoy!

Neapolitan Creamsicles

Prep time: 20 minutes (+4-6 hours)

Cooking time: none

Servings: 10

Nutrients per serving:

Carbohydrates – 25.4 g

Fat – 9 g

Protein – 3.3 g

Calories – 188

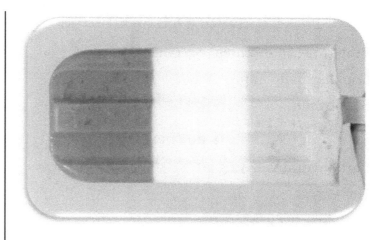

Ingredients:

- 1 cup plain low-fat Greek yogurt
- ¾ cup granulated sugar
- 1 cup heavy cream
- 8 oz fresh strawberries
- 1 tsp vanilla extract
- 3 Tbsp unsweetened cocoa powder
- 1 tbsp milk

Instructions:

1. Whisk together Greek yogurt, sugar, cream and vanilla extract in a bowl until sugar is completely dissolved. Divide the yogurt mixture into three portions.
2. Puree strawberries until smooth.
3. Add a ½ cup of the yogurt mixture and blend again, about 1 minute.
4. Whisk together 1 cup yogurt mixture with 3 tbsp cocoa powder in a bowl .
5. Add ½ tbsp milk and stir well. Pour this mixture into molds. Freeze 5-10 minutes.
6. Whip the remaining yogurt mixture and ½ tbsp milk.
7. Remove molds from the freezer. Pour the white mixture over the chocolate mixture. Freeze 5-10 minutes.
8. Remove molds from the freezer. Pour the strawberry mixture over the white mixture.
9. Add sticks and freeze for at least 5 hours.

Mint Chocolate Chip Yogurt

Prep time: 15 minutes (+4-6 hours)

Cooking time: none

Servings: 6

Nutrients per serving:

Carbohydrates – 42.5 g

Fat – 75 g

Protein – 7.4 g

Calories – 421

Ingredients:

For the popsicles:

- 2 cups vanilla Greek-style yogurt
- ½ cup milk
- 1-2 tsp mint extract
- 2 tbsps honey
- ½ cup chocolate chips
- Green food coloring

For the topping:

- 1 cup milk chocolate bar
- 1 tsp vanilla extract
- 2 tbsp coconut oil

Instructions:

For the popsicles:

1. Whisk together all ingredients except the chocolate chips.
2. Stir in chocolate chips.
3. Pour the mixture into popsicle molds. Freeze for 2 hours.
4. Add sticks and freeze for at least 4 hours.

For the topping:

5. Melt milk chocolate in a microwave. add coconut oil and stir every 20 seconds.
6. Add the vanilla extract, stirring. Set aside to cool for 5-10 minutes.
7. When popsicles are completely frozen, dunk each pop into chocolate. Enjoy!

Orange Homemade

Prep time: 15 minutes (+4-6 hours)

Cooking time: none

Servings: 10

Nutrients per serving:

Carbohydrates – 22.8 g

Fat – 6.7 g

Protein – 2.7 g

Calories – 162

Ingredients:

- 3 cups freshly-squeezed orange juice
- 4 cups vanilla ice cream

Instructions:

1. Spoon one tablespoon of ice cream into the molds.
2. Pour orange juice into each mold, almost to the top.
3. Freeze for 2 hours.
4. Add sticks and freeze for at least 4 hours.

Fruity Pebbles Yogurt

Prep time: 15 minutes (+4-6 hours)

Cooking time: none

Servings: 8

Nutrients per serving:

Carbohydrates – 5.9 g

Fat – 0.4 g

Protein – 3.7 g

Calories – 44

Ingredients:

- 1½ cups fat-free Greek yogurt
- ¾ cup 1% milk
- 1 cup Fruity Pebbles, divided

Instructions:

1. Blend yogurt and milk in a blender until creamy.
2. Stir in ¾ cup Fruity Pebbles.
3. Put ¼ cup Fruity Pebbles into the bottoms of the molds.
4. Pour the yogurt-milk mixture into the molds.
5. Add sticks and freeze at least 4-6 hours.

BERRY POPSICLES

Dragon Fruit and Strawberry Cream

Prep time: 15 minutes (+6 hours)

Cooking time: none

Servings: 6-8

Nutrients per serving:

Carbohydrates – 18.4 g

Fat – 1.9 g

Protein – 6.8 g

Calories – 115

Ingredients:

- 2 oz frozen pitaya
- 1 cup strawberries
- ½ cup apple juice
- 4 tbsp honey
- 1 cup canned coconut milk or cream
- ½ cup 0% fat coconut Greek yogurt
- 2 scoops collagen peptides/vital proteins

Instructions:

1. Puree pitaya , strawberries, apple juice, and 2 tbsp honey in a blender. Pour into a jar.
2. To prepare coconut cream: combine coconut milk, Greek yogurt, 2 tbsp honey, and collagen peptides in a blender until creamy and smooth.
3. Alternately pour fruit mixture and coconut cream into popsicle molds.
4. Add sticks and freeze approximately 6 hours.

Berry Mojito

Prep time: 1 hour 30 minutes (+4-6 hours)

Cooking time: none

Servings: 10

Nutrients per serving:

Carbohydrates – 10.6 g

Fat – 0.2 g

Protein – 0.5 g

Calories – 42

Ingredients:

- 1 cup blackberry puree
- 1 cup blueberry puree
- 1 cup raspberry puree
- ½ cup lime juice
- 3 tbsp honey
- ¼ cup mint leaves

Instructions:

1. Combine honey, lime juice, and mint in a blender until mint is well minced.
2. In three separate bowls, combine 2 tbsp of liquid and each of the berry purees.
3. Add raspberry puree in popsicle molds first and freeze for 15-30 minutes.
4. Remove molds from freezer and add blueberry puree. Freeze for 20-30 minutes.
5. Remove molds from the freezer and add blackberry puree plus sticks. Freeze 4-6 hours till full firm.

Strawberry Sweet Tea

Prep time: 20 minutes (+3-4 hours)

Cooking time: none

Servings: 10-15

Nutrients per serving:

Carbohydrates – 19.9 g

Fat – 0.1 g

Protein – 0.3 g

Calories – 76

Ingredients:

- 1 cup granulated sugar
- 8 cups water
- 2 family size tea bags
- 3 cups strawberries
- Juice of 1 lemon

Instructions:

1. Bring water to boil, then remove from heat.
2. Put tea bags in hot water and let steep 5-6 minutes.
3. Puree 2 cups of strawberries and lemon juice in a blender.
4. Push the puree through a sieve.
5. Add the mixture to the hot tea mixture and stir.
6. Add the sugar to the tea-strawberry mixture and stir until the sugar is completely dissolved.
7. Slice the remaining strawberries and put some slices to each mold.
8. Cool the strawberry-tea mixture to room temperature and fill the molds.
9. Add sticks and freeze for at least 3-4 hours.

Strawberry Popsicles

Prep time: 30 minutes (+3-6 hours)

Cooking time: none

Servings: 4

Nutrients per serving:

Carbohydrates – 15.9 g

Fat – 0.1 g

Protein – 0.3 g

Calories – 60

Ingredients:

- 1 cup fresh strawberries
- ¼ cup sugar
- 1 tbsp lime juice

Instructions:

1. Chop strawberries into pieces and sprinkle with sugar. Set aside for 20 minutes.
2. Add lime juice and mash strawberries with a fork until smooth.
3. Pour the strawberry mixture into the molds, add sticks and freeze for at least 3-6 hours.

Raspberry Lemon Yogurt

Prep time: 15 minutes (+4-6 hours)

Cooking time: none

Servings: 6

Nutrients per serving:

Carbohydrates – 18.9 g

Fat – 56.5 g

Protein – 3.6 g

Calories – 141

Ingredients:

- 2 cups vanilla Greek-style yogurt
- 1 cup fresh raspberries
- Juice and zest of 1 lemon
- 2 tbsp honey

Instructions:

1. Combine raspberries and honey in a blender. Pour mixture into a bowl.
2. Mix vanilla yogurt and lemon juice and zest.
3. Stir in the raspberry mixture and blend for 1-2 minutes on medium speed.
4. Pour into the molds, add sticks and freeze for at least 4-6 hours.

Three Ingredient Strawberry

Prep time: 15 minutes (+4-6 hours)

Cooking time: none

Servings: 10

Nutrients per serving:

Carbohydrates – 12.1 g

Fat – 0.2 g

Protein – 0.5 g

Calories – 46

Ingredients:

- 4 cups fresh strawberries
- Zest and flesh of 1 lime
- ¼ cup honey

Instructions:

1. Puree strawberries, honey, lime zest and lime flesh in a blender until totally smooth.
2. Pour the mixture into popsicle molds. Freeze for 2 hours.
3. Add sticks and freeze for at least 4 hours.

Strawberries and Cream

Prep time: 15 minutes (+4-6 hours)

Cooking time: none

Servings: 8

Nutrients per serving:

Carbohydrates – 23.1 g

Fat – 9.2 g

Protein – 1.3 g

Calories – 168

Ingredients:

- 1 lb strawberries
- 1½ cups full-fat coconut milk
- ½ cup honey
- 1 tsp vanilla extract

Instructions:

1. Puree strawberries and ¼ cup honey in a blender.
2. In a bowl, mix coconut milk, ¼ cup honey, and vanilla extract.
3. Pour 1-2 tbsp of the strawberry puree into the molds, then 1-2 tbsp of the coconut mixture. Layer until the molds are filled.
4. Freeze for 2 hours.
5. Add sticks and freeze for at least 4 hours.

Blueberries & Cream

Prep time: 5 minutes (+4-6 hours)

Cooking time: none

Servings: 12

Nutrients per serving:

Carbohydrates – 19.1 g

Fat – 15 g

Protein – 1 g

Calories – 205

Ingredients:

- 12 oz fresh blueberries
- 1 pint heavy cream
- ¼ cup water
- ¾ cup granulated sugar

Instructions:

1. Blend blueberries, water, and ¼ cup sugar in a blender until smooth mixture. Set aside.
2. Whisk heavy whipping cream and ½ cup sugar gently in a large bowl until the sugar is completely dissolved.
3. Pour the blueberry mixture then cream mixture into the molds until all the mixtures have been used.
4. Freeze for 2 hours.
5. Add sticks and freeze for at least 4 hours.

Blueberry Cheese-Cake

Prep time: 10 minutes (+4-6 hours)

Cooking time: none

Servings: 6

Nutrients per serving:

Carbohydrates – 13.2 g

Fat – 0.8 g

Protein – 3.5 g

Calories – 73

Ingredients:

- 1½ cups frozen blueberries, thawed
- ½ cup low-fat cottage cheese
- ½ cup low-fat milk
- 3 tbsp maple syrup
- 1 tsp lemon juice
- ½ tsp vanilla extract
- ⅛ tsp ground cinnamon

Instructions:

1. Puree all ingredients in a blender until smooth.
2. Freeze for 2 hours.
3. Add sticks and freeze for at least 4 hours.

Blueberry Sour Cream

Prep time: 10 minutes (+6 hours)

Cooking time: none

Servings: 4

Nutrients per serving:

Carbohydrates – 10.3 g

Fat – 9.9 g

Protein – 1.8 g

Calories – 132

Ingredients:

- 1 cup frozen blueberries, thawed
- ½ cup sour cream
- ¾ cup unsweetened vanilla almond milk
- 1-2 drops vanilla stevia drop, to taste

Instructions:

1. In a bowl, whisk together sour cream and vanilla almond milk.
2. Stir in blueberries gently.
3. Add vanilla stevia.
4. Pour the mixture into the molds. Freeze for 30 minutes.
5. Add sticks and freeze for at least 6 hours.

Raspberry Cheesecake

Prep time: 45 minutes (+4-6 hours)

Cooking time: 10 minutes

Servings: 6

Nutrients per serving:

Carbohydrates – 12.7 g

Fat – 0.7 g

Protein – 3.4 g

Calories – 70

Ingredients:

- 8 oz fresh raspberries
- 1 tbsp water
- 4 oz low-fat cream cheese
- 3 tbsp fat-free milk
- ⅓ cup powdered sugar
- 1 tsp vanilla extract

Instructions:

1. Combine raspberries and water in a saucepan over medium heat, about 10 minutes.
2. Puree the berry mixture in a blender.
3. Cool in the fridge for 30 minutes.
4. Combine cream cheese, milk, vanilla extract, and powdered sugar in a blender until smooth.
5. Alternately spoon cream cheese mixture and berry puree into the molds.
6. Add sticks and freeze for at least 4-6 hours.

VEGGIE POPSICLES

Tomato Strawberry Basil

Prep time: 10 minutes (+6 hours)

Cooking time: none

Servings: 8

Nutrients per serving:

Carbohydrates – 5 g

Fat – 0 g

Protein – 1 g

Calories – 25

Ingredients:

- 8 cherry tomatoes
- 20 strawberries
- 12 basil leaves
- 4 tbsp lime juice
- 2 tsp maple syrup

Instructions:

1. Combine all ingredients in a blender until smooth.
2. Pour mixture into the molds. Freeze for 30 minutes.
3. Add sticks and freeze for at least 6 hours.

Red Pepper Mango Berry

Prep time: 10 minutes (+6 hours)

Cooking time: none

Servings: 8

Nutrients per serving:

Carbohydrates – 16.7 g

Fat – 0.3 g

Protein – 1 g

Calories – 67

Ingredients:

- 1 cup blueberries
- 1 cup of red chard
- ½ red pepper, seedless, chopped
- 1 banana
- 1 cup apple juice

Instructions:

1. Combine all ingredients in a blender until the smooth.
2. Pour the mixture into the molds. Freeze for 30 minutes.
3. Add sticks and freeze for at least 6 hours.

Carrot Orange Mango

Prep time: 10 minutes (+3-4 hours)

Cooking time: none

Servings: 5-6

Nutrients per serving:

Carbohydrates – 12.2 g

Fat – 0.3 g

Protein – 0.8 g

Calories – 50

Ingredients:

- ½ cup carrot juice
- ½ cup orange juice
- 1½ cup mango

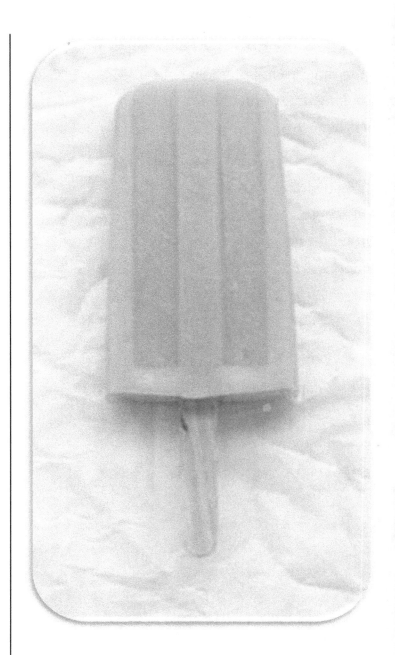

Instructions:

1. Blend all ingredients until smooth.
2. Pour into molds, add sticks and freeze at least 3-4 hours.

Beet Strawberry

Prep time: 10 minutes (+3-4 hours)

Cooking time: none

Servings: 5-6

Nutrients per serving:

Carbohydrates – 10 g

Fat – 0.2 g

Protein – 0.5 g

Calories – 41

Ingredients:

- ¾ cup apple juice
- 1½ cups strawberries
- 1 tsp lemon juice or balsamic vinegar
- ½ cup beets, cooked and cooled

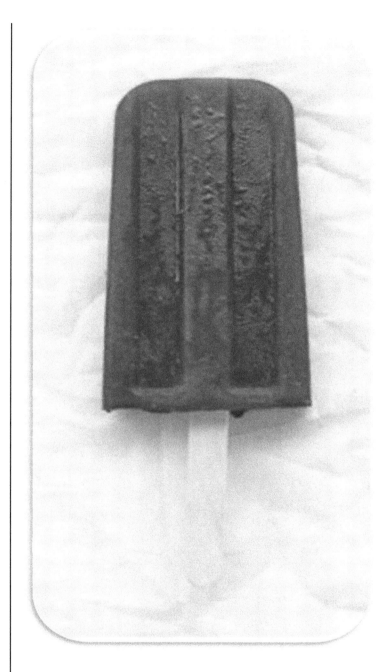

Instructions:

1. Blend all ingredients until smooth.
2. Pour into molds, add sticks and freeze 3-4 hours.

Spinach Creamy Lime

Prep time: 10 minutes (+3-4 hours)

Cooking time: none

Servings: 5-6

Nutrients per serving:

Carbohydrates – 12.7 g

Fat – 8.7 g

Protein – 1.4 g

Calories – 123

Ingredients:

- 1½ cups pineapple
- ½ banana
- ¾ cup coconut milk
- ½-1 cup spinach
- Zest and juice of 1 lime

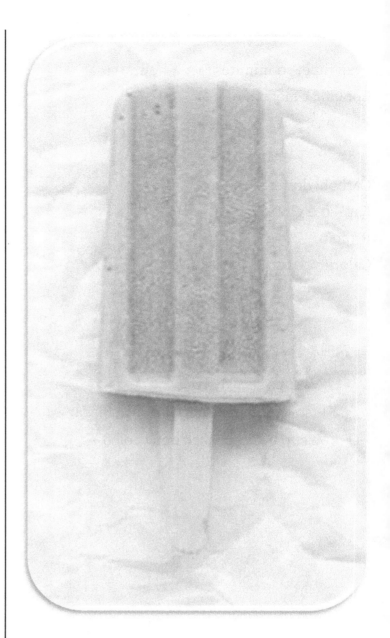

Instructions:

1. Puree all ingredients in a high-powered blender for 5-6 minutes until totally smooth.
2. Pour into molds, add sticks and freeze 3-4 hours.

Creamed Corn

Prep time: 10 minutes (+4-6 hours)

Cooking time: none

Servings: 4

Nutrients per serving:

Carbohydrates – 16 g

Fat – 1.8 g

Protein – 1 g

Calories – 77

Ingredients:

- 5 oz cooked corn kernels
- 12 oz unsweetened coconut milk ()
- Pinch of sea salt
- 1-2 tbsps honey

Instructions:

1. Blend all ingredients in a blender until mostly smooth.
2. Pour the mixture into the molds. Freeze for 30 minutes..
3. Add sticks and freeze for at least 4-6 hours.

Carrot Blueberry Yogurt

Prep time: 15 minutes (+4-6 hours)

Cooking time: none

Servings: 6

Nutrients per serving:

Carbohydrates – 20 g

Fat – 0.2 g

Protein – 5 g

Calories – 97

Ingredients:

- 1½ cups blueberries
- ½ cup carrot juice
- 1½ cups fat-free, plain Greek yogurt
- ¼ cup honey

Instructions:

1. Whisk together carrot juice, yogurt, and honey.
2. Stir in blueberries gently.
3. Pour the mixture into the molds. Freeze for 30 minutes..
4. Add sticks and freeze for at least 4-6 hours.

Avocado Chocolate

Prep time: 10 minutes (+4-6 hours)

Cooking time: none

Servings: 10

Nutrients per serving:

Carbohydrates – 21.9 g

Fat – 18.6 g

Protein – 4.5 g

Calories – 264

Ingredients:

- 3 avocados
- 1½ cups milk
- 4 tablespoons sweetened condensed milk
- 1-2 tablespoons simple syrup or agave syrup

For the topping:

- 4 oz dark chocolate

Instructions:

1. Puree avocados, milk and sweetened condensed milk in a blender or food processor until smooth.
2. Add simple syrup or agave syrup if it is not sweet enough.
3. Pour the mixture into popsicle molds. Freeze for 2 hours.
4. Add sticks and freeze for at least 4 hours.

For the topping:

5. Melt dark chocolate in a microwave, stirring every 20 seconds.
6. When popsicles are completely frozen,dunk each pop into chocolate. Enjoy!

Recipe Note

The avocado mixture can be quite thick. Add more milk to thin.

POPSICLES for ADULTS

Root Beer

Prep time: 10 minutes (+3.5 hours)

Cooking time: none

Servings: 12-14

Nutrients per serving:

Carbohydrates – 12.4 g

Fat – 4.6 g

Protein – 2.2 g

Calories – 99

Ingredients:

- 1 cup heavy cream
- 1 cup whole milk
- 4 large egg yolks
- ⅓ cup brown sugar
- 1 tsp vanilla extract
- pinch of salt
- 16 fl oz root beer

Instructions:

1. In a heavy pot on medium heat, heat the cream and milk, stirring, approximately 5 minutes.
2. In a heat-resistant bowl, beat the egg yolks, sugar, vanilla, and salt until the volume of the mixture doubles, about 2 minutes.
3. Pour half of warm cream mixture into yolk mixture, whisking until smooth.
4. Pour the mix into a pot and set it to medium heat.
5. Stir with a wooden spoon until the mixture is thick enough to cover the back of the spoon for 1 to 2 minutes. Do not let boil.
6. Push through a fine sieve and completely cool over an ice bath.
7. Fill molds ¼ with full vanilla custard and freeze for about 30 minutes.
8. Pour in the root beer until molds are half full, then freeze about 30 minutes.
9. Add remaining vanilla custard until the form is full ¾.
10. Place sticks in molds and freeze for 1 hour until they are completely solid.
11. Fill the forms with remaining root beer . Freeze for at least 2.5 hours.

Recipe Note

Open the bottle of root beer at least 30 minutes before using.

Melon Basil

Prep time: 10 minutes (+4-6 hour)

Cooking time: none

Servings: 10

Nutrients per serving:

Carbohydrates – 19.7 g

Fat – 0.1 g

Protein – 0.5 g

Calories – 92

Ingredients:

- 1 lb cantaloupe
- 5-7 mint leaves
- 6 oz Tequila Reposado
- 4 oz limeade
- 4 oz ginger beer
- 2 oz simple syrup (less if the melon is ripe and sweet)

Instructions:

1. Add cantaloupe, mint leaves, Tequila, and limeade to a blender and process until smooth.
2. Add the ginger beer and mix to combine.
3. Add 1 tablespoon of simple syrup at a time to sweeten the mixture.
4. Pour mixture into the popsicle mold.
5. Cover molds with foil, then make small holes in the center of each mold. Insert popsicle stick and transfer popsicle molds to the freezer.
6. Freeze for 4 to 6 hours.

Tinto De Verano Red Wine

Prep time: 15 minutes (+4 hours)

Cooking time: 5 minutes

Servings: 10

Nutrients per serving:

Carbohydrates – 9.3 g

Fat – 0 g

Protein – 0.1 g

Calories – 57

Ingredients:

- ¼ cup granulated sugar
- ¼ cup filtered water
- Juice of 1 lime
- 1¼ cups red wine
- 1¼ cups lemon-lime soda

Instructions:

1. Combine sugar and filtered water in a small pot. Heat on medium or medium-high heat until the sugar is completely dissolved.
2. Remove from heat and mix with lime juice. Set aside to cool.
3. Combine wine and lemon-lime soda. Then stir in cooled lime syrup.
4. Divide the liquid between the molds, leaving some space at the top.
5. Freeze for 4 hours.

Recipe Note

Use half of the simple syrup and two extra tablespoons of wine and soda for a less sweet popsicle.

Sparkling Champagne

Prep time: 5 minutes (+3 hours)

Cooking time: none

Servings: 6-8

Nutrients per serving:

Carbohydrates – 23.5 g

Fat – 0 g

Protein – 0.2 g

Calories – 155

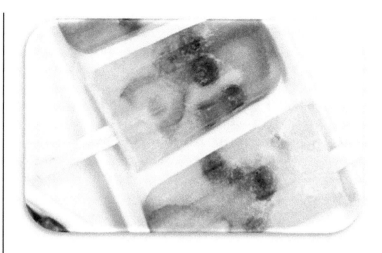

Ingredients:

- 1 bottle Champagne
- ¼-½ cup agave syrup
- 3 cups mixed berries (strawberry, blueberry, raspberry)
- 8-10 leaves basil or fresh mint

Instructions:

1. Place some berries and mint/basil into the molds.
2. Fill the molds with the Champagne, leaving ¼ inch at the top of the molds.
3. Add sticks and freeze 3 hours.

Strawberries & Cream Tequila

Prep time: 10 minutes (+4 hours)

Cooking time: 2-3 minutes

Servings: 11

Nutrients per serving:

Carbohydrates – 12.5 g

Fat – 7.3 g

Protein – 2.2 g

Calories – 126

Ingredients:

- ¼ cup Patron Silver tequila
- 8 oz strawberries
- ⅔ cup powdered sugar
- 1 tsp vanilla extract
- 1½ cups sour cream
- 1½ cups 2% or whole milk

Instructions:

1. Combine the strawberries, powdered sugar and vanilla extract in a saucepan.
2. Bring to a boil, then let simmer until it thickens. Remove from heat and mush the strawberries with the fork. Let it cool completely.
3. Mix cooled strawberries with milk, tequila, and sour cream, whisking well.
4. Pour the mixture into the popsicle forms, leaving about ¼ inches at the top.
5. Insert popsicle sticks and freeze for at least 4 hours.
6. Remove gently as these are softer because of the alcohol.

Gin, Basil and Mango

Prep time: 5 minutes (+1 hour)

Cooking time: none

Servings: 6

Nutrients per serving:

Carbohydrates – 16.3 g

Fat – 0.3 g

Protein – 0.6 g

Calories – 112

Ingredients:

- 1 large mango
- 1 bunch basil
- ½-⅓ cup gin
- 2-3 tbsp maple syrup
- Juice of 1 lime

Instructions:

1. Put all ingredients in a blender and blend until smooth.
2. Pour into molds and insert sticks. Freeze overnight.

Sparkling Fruit Izze & Cream Cocktail

Prep time: 5 minutes (+12 hours)

Cooking time: none

Servings: 4-6

Nutrients per serving:

Carbohydrates – 7.1 g

Fat – 6.7 g

Protein – 0 g

Calories – 116

Ingredients:

- 1 tbsp honey
- ½ cup heavy cream
- 10 oz sparkling Izze Soda, any flavor
- 2 ounces vodka, plain or flavored

Instructions:

1. Whisk together all ingredients.
2. Pour into popsicle molds.
3. Add sticks and freeze overnight.

CONCLUSION

Thank you for reading this book and having the patience to try the recipes.

I do hope that you have had as much enjoyment reading and experimenting with the meals as I have had writing the book.

If you would like to leave a comment, you can do so at the Order section->Digital orders, in your account.

Stay safe and healthy!

Recipe Index

Conversion Tables

VOLUME EQUIVALENTS (LIQUID)

US STANDARD	US STANDARD (OUNCES)	METRIC
2 tablespoons	1 fl. oz.	30 mL
¼ cup	2 fl. oz.	60 mL
½ cup	4 fl. oz.	120 mL
1 cup	8 fl. oz.	240mL
1½ cups	12 fl. oz.	355 mL
2 cups or 1 pint	16 fl. oz.	475 mL
4 cups or 1 quart	32 fl. oz.	1 L
1 gallon	128 fl. oz.	4 L

OVEN TEMPERATURES

FAHRENHEIT (°F)	CELSIUS (°C) APPROXIMATE
250 °F	120 °C
300 °F	150 °C
325 °F	165 °C
350 °F	180 °C
375 °F	190 °C
400 °F	200 °C
425 °F	220 °C
450 °F	230 °C

VOLUME EQUIVALENTS (LIQUID)

US STANDARD	METRIC (APPROXIMATE)
1/8 teaspoon	0.5 mL
¼ teaspoon	1 mL
½ teaspoon	2 mL
2/3 teaspoon	4 mL
1 teaspoon	5 mL
1 tablespoon	15 mL
¼ cup	59 mL
1/3 cup	79 mL
½ cup	118 mL
2/3 cup	156 mL
¾ cup	177 mL
1 cup	235 mL
2 cups or 1 pint	475 mL
3 cups	700 mL
4 cups or 1 quart	1 L
½ gallon	2 L
1 gallon	4 L

WEIGHT EQUIVALENTS

US STANDARD	METRIC (APPROXIMATE)
½ ounce	15 g
1 ounce	30 g
2 ounces	60 g
4 ounces	115 g
8 ounces	225 g
12 ounces	340 g
16 ounces or 1 pound	455 g

Other Books by Kaitlyn Donnelly